TWENTYSIX HOUSES ALONG WALDEGGSTRASSE

OTTO HAINZL

1 9 6 6

TWENTYSIX HOUSES ALONG WALDEGGSTRASSE
BY OTTO HAINZL 2022
www.ottohainzl.at

© 2022 KEHRER VERLAG HEIDELBERG
© 2022 OTTO HAINZL
© VG BILD-KUNST, BONN 2022

FIRST EDITION, 2022, 400 COPIES
Thanks to all supporters of this work
and to Ed Ruscha

PRINTED & BOUND IN GERMANY
ISBN 978-3-96900-101-1

www.kehrerverlag.com

TO THE FORMER RESIDENTS
OF WALDEGGSTRASSE
WHOSE HOUSES,
KEPT VACANT FOR TWO DECADES,
WILL GIVE WAY TO A THROUGH ROAD

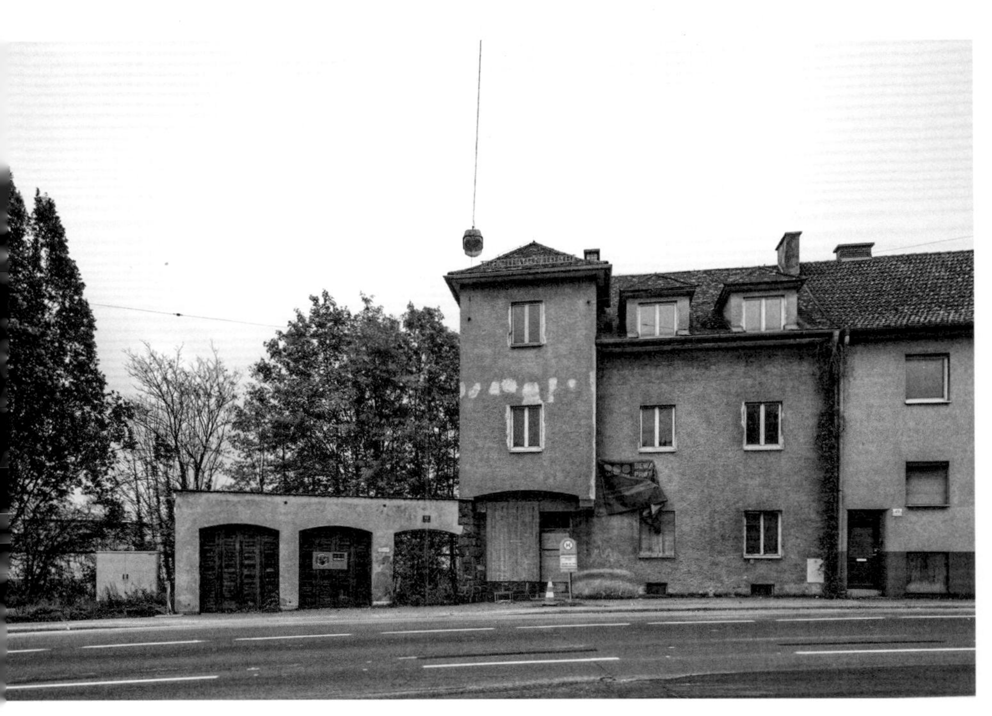

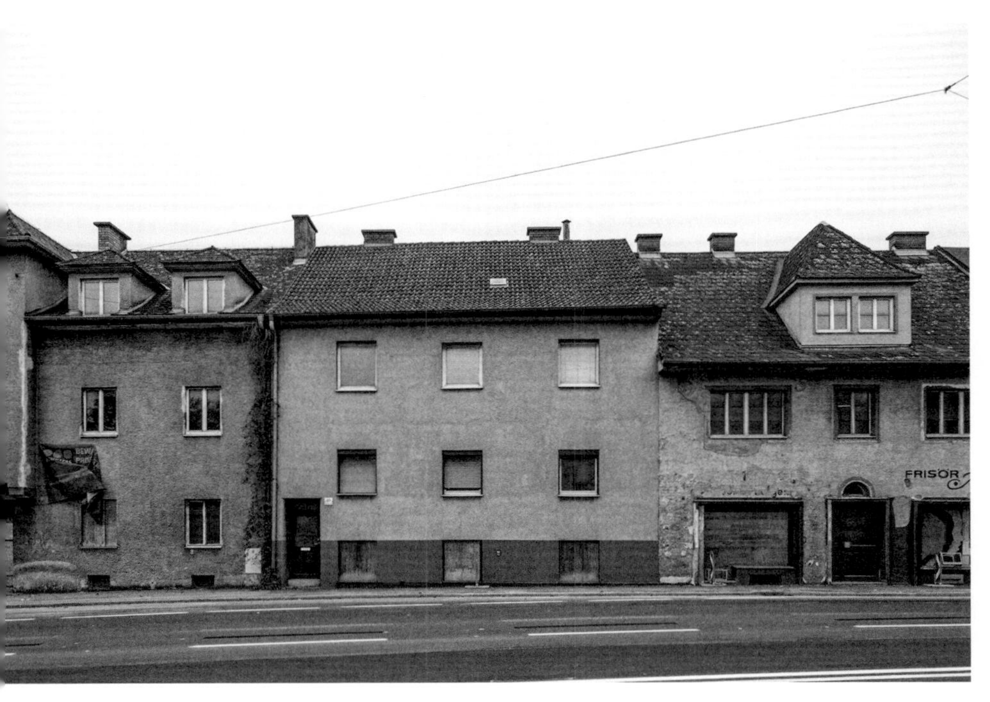

BEW
FRISÖR

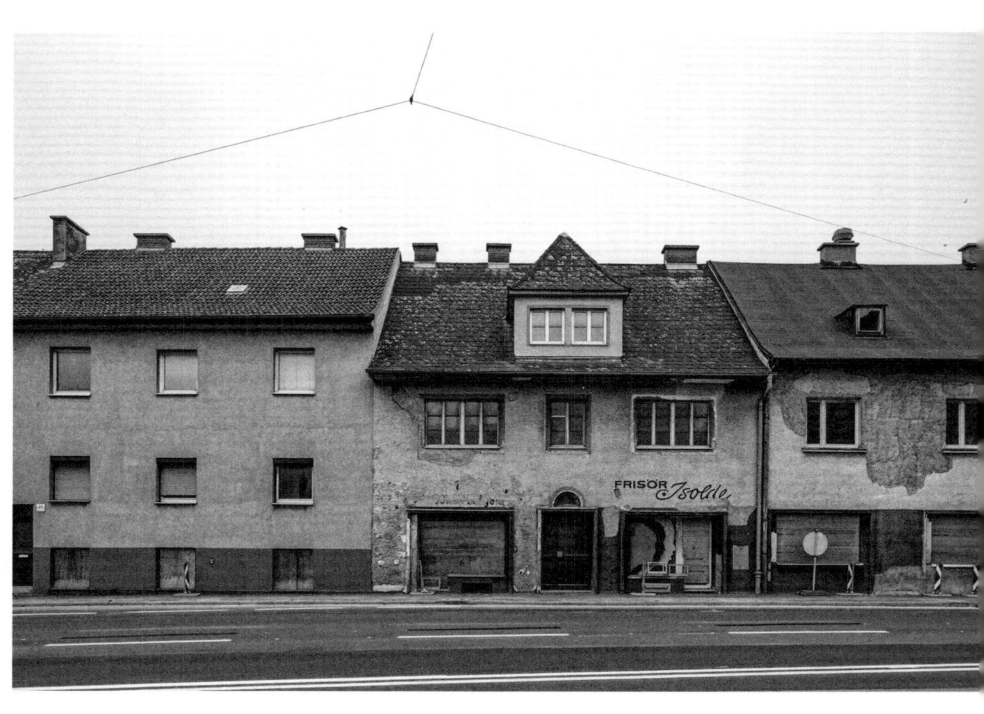

FRISÖR Isolde

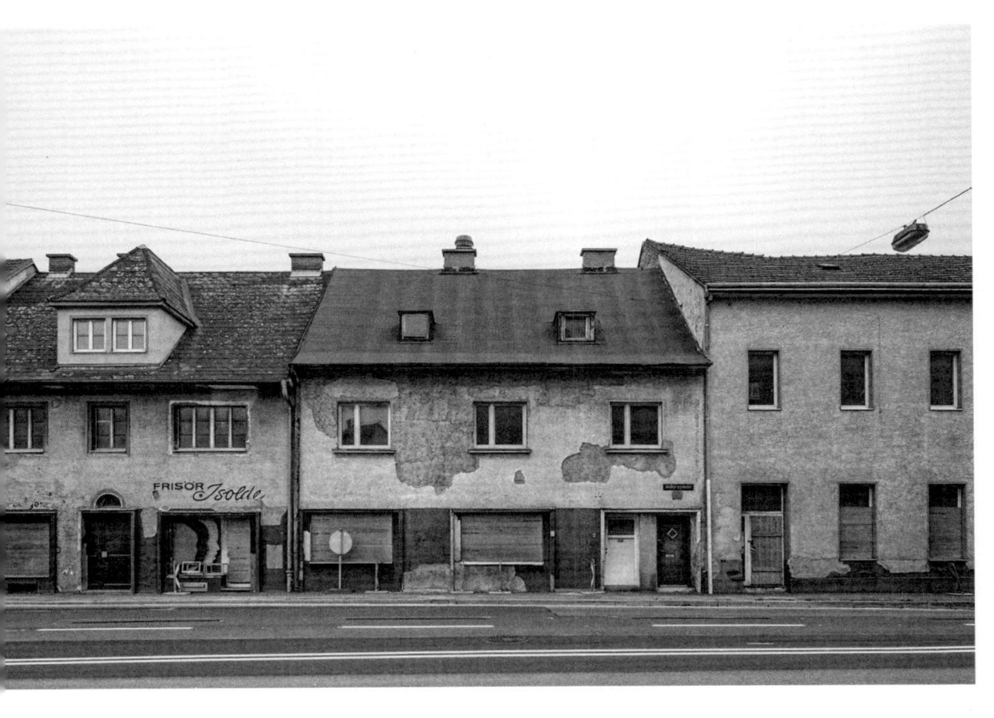
FRISÖR Isolde

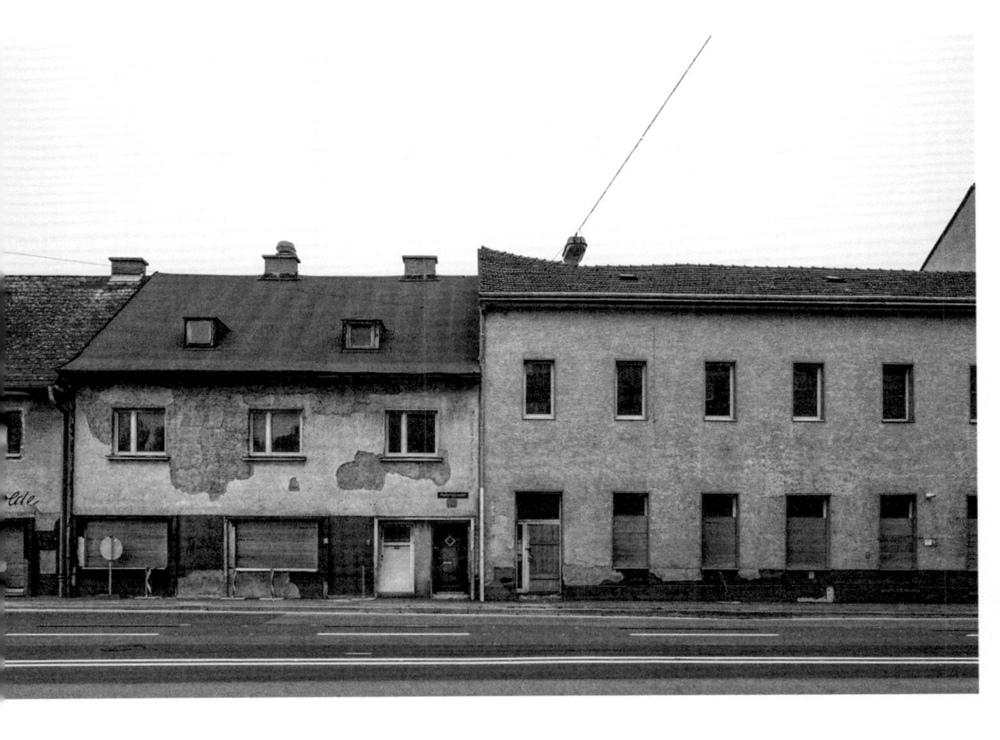

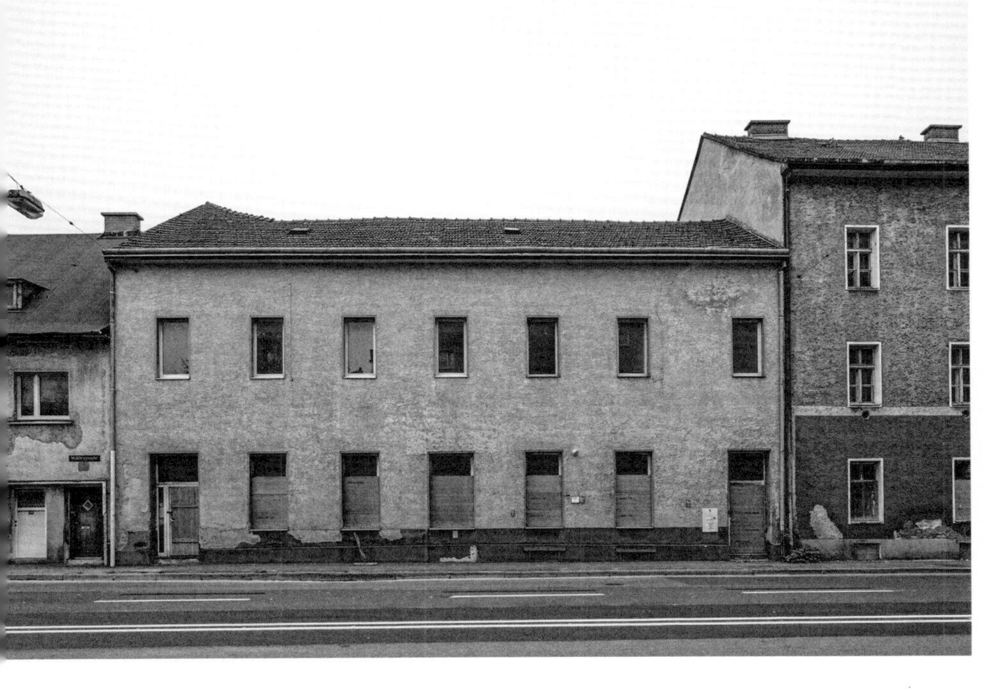

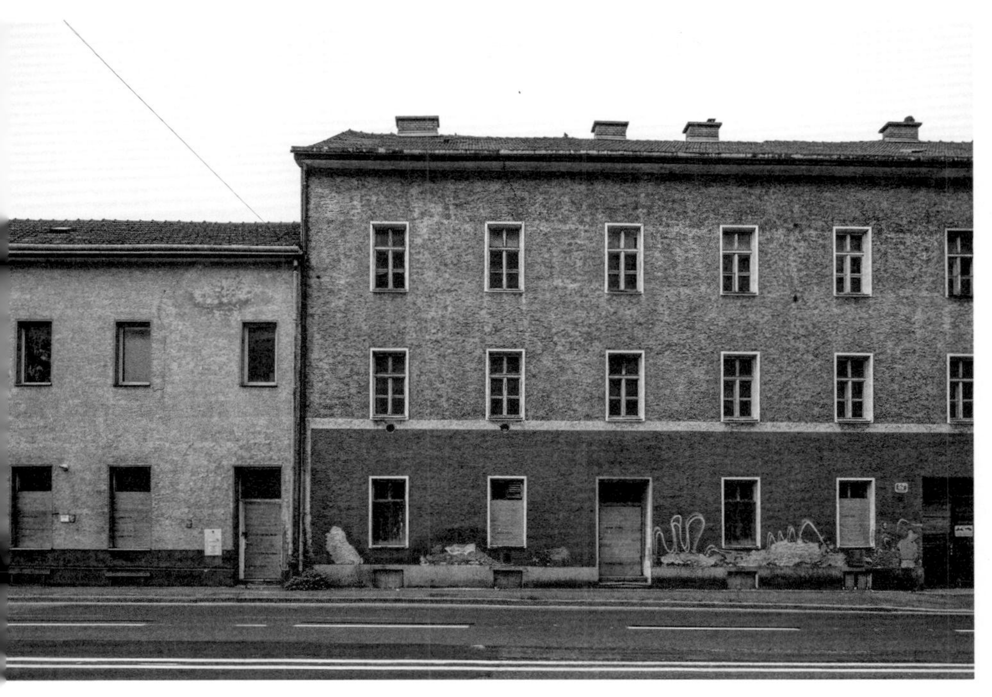

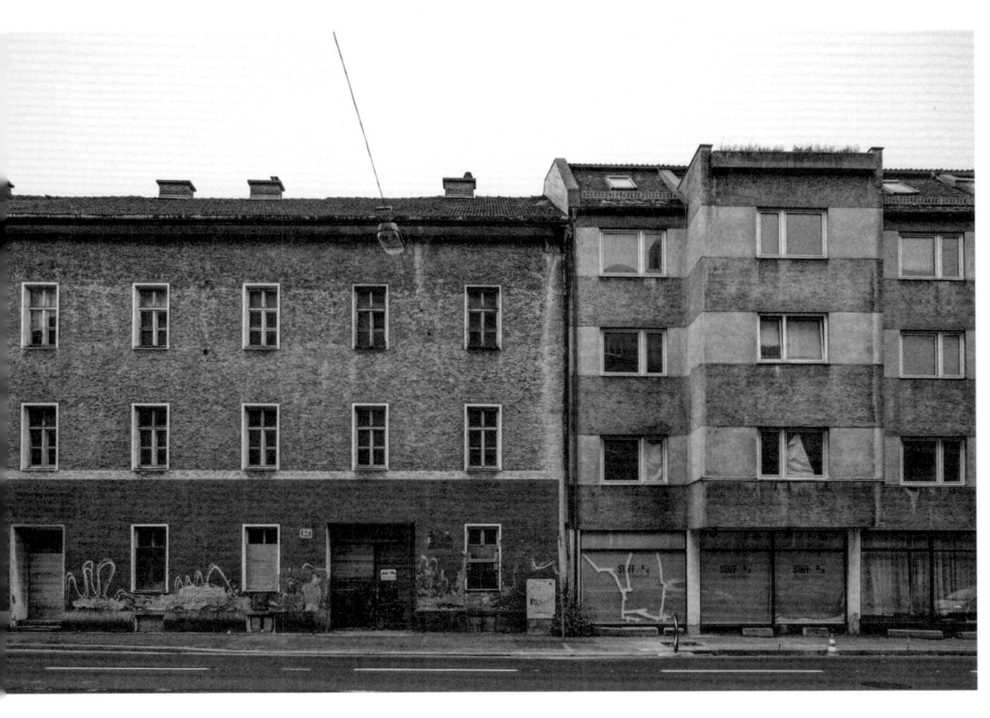

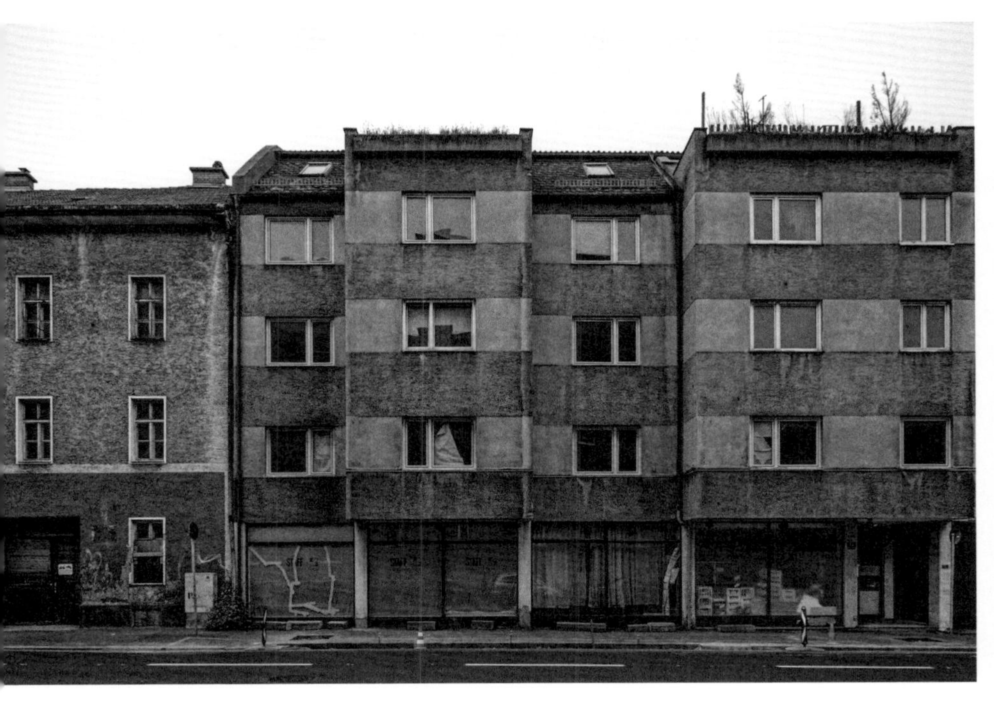

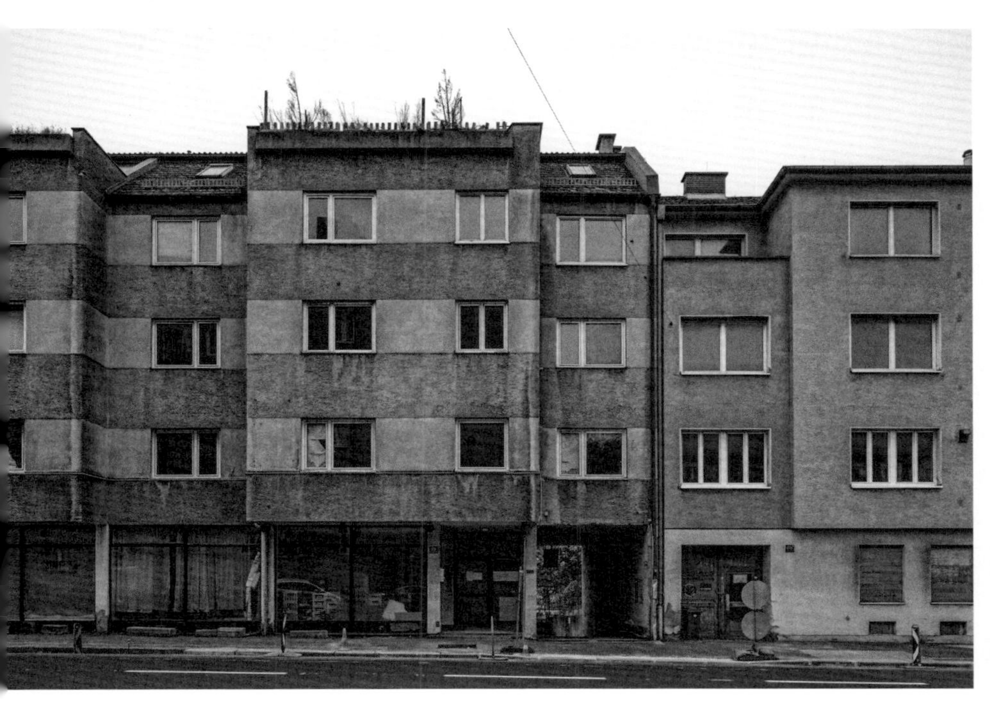

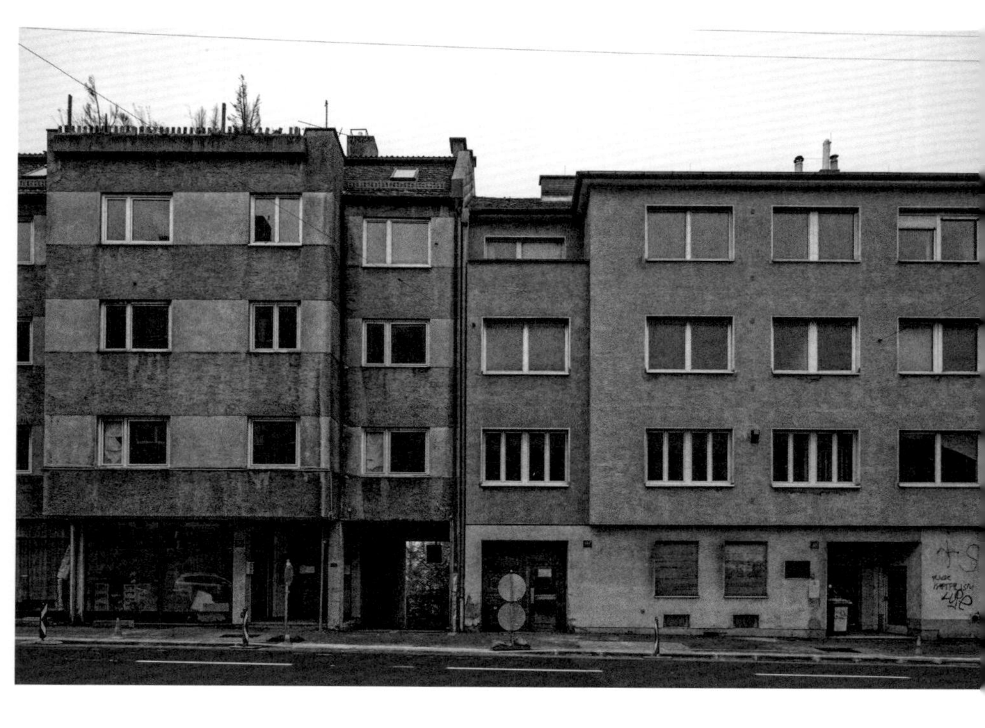

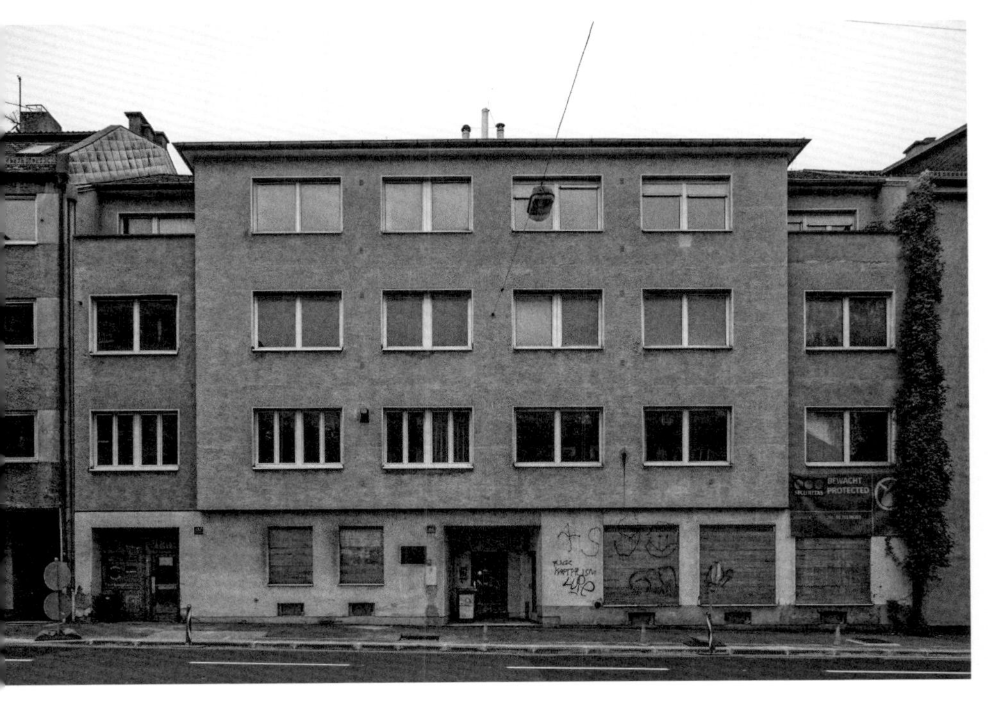

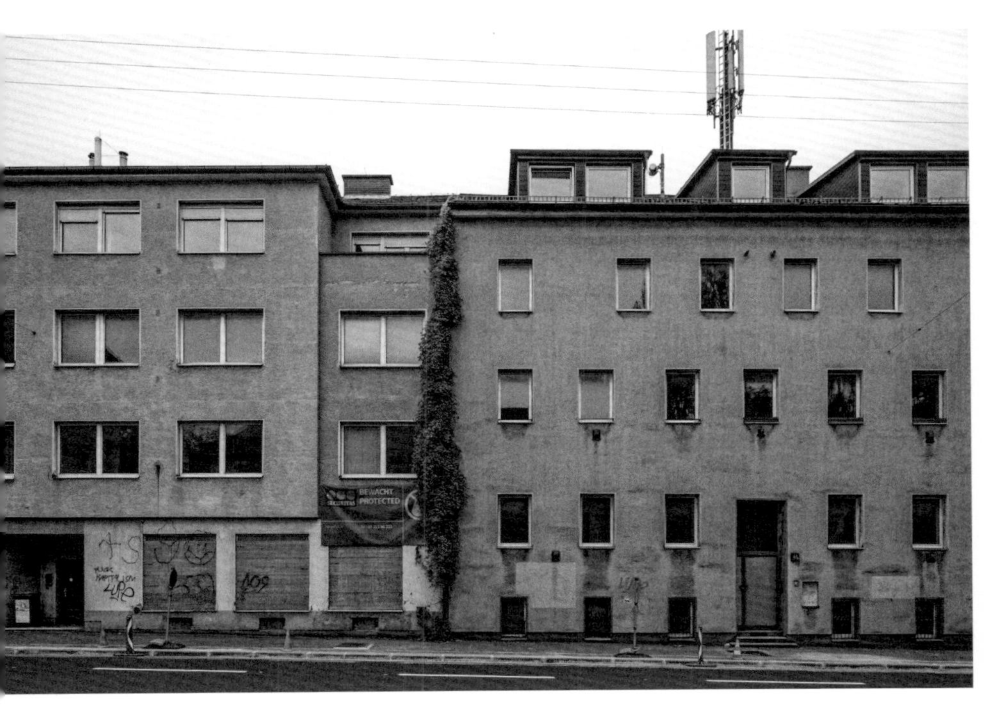

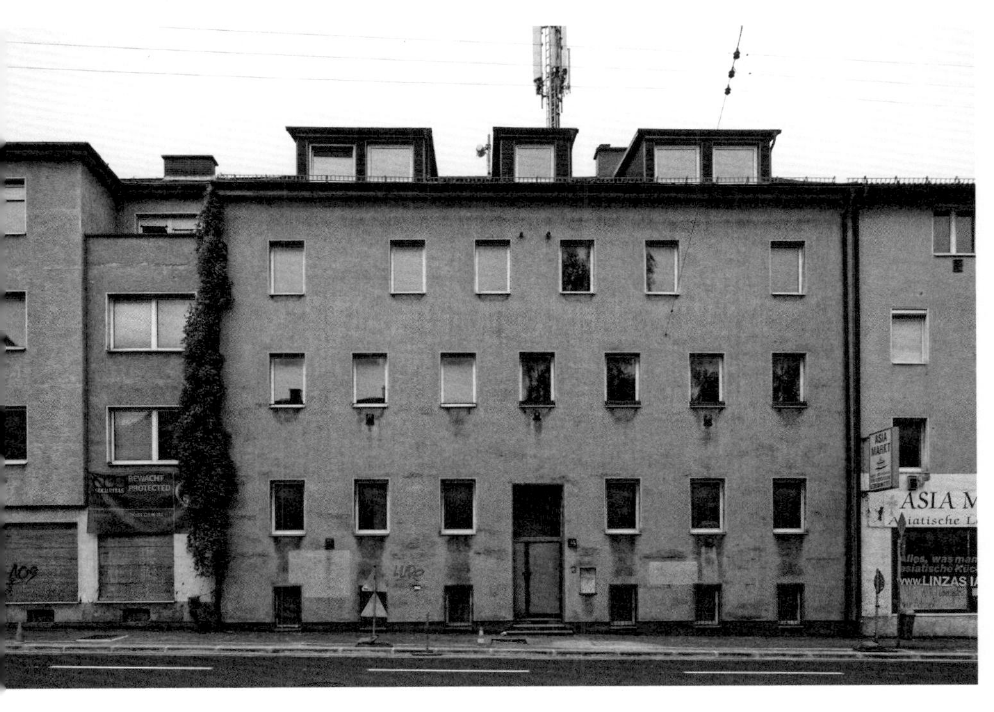

BEWACHT
PROTECTED
SECURITAS
ASIA
MARKT
ASIA M
Asiatische L
Alles, was man
asiatische Küc
www.LINZAS IA

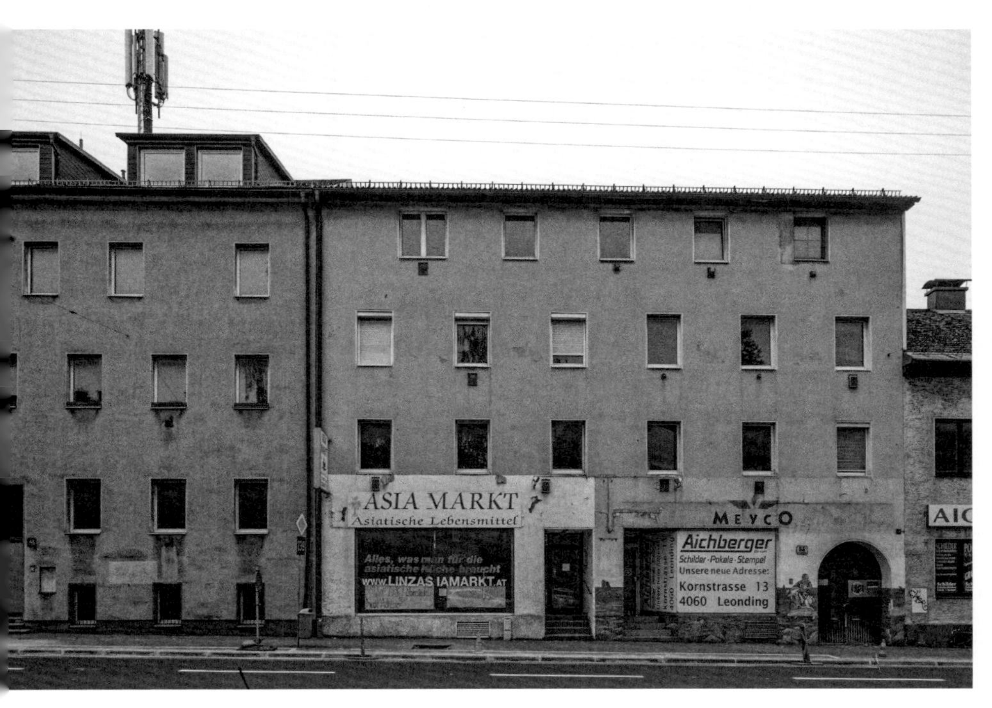
ASIA MARKT
Asiatische Lebensmittel
Alles, was man für die
asiatische Küche braucht
www.LINZASIAMARKT.AT
MEYCO
Aichberger
Schilder · Pokale · Stempel
Unsere neue Adresse:
Kornstrasse 13
4060 Leonding
AIC

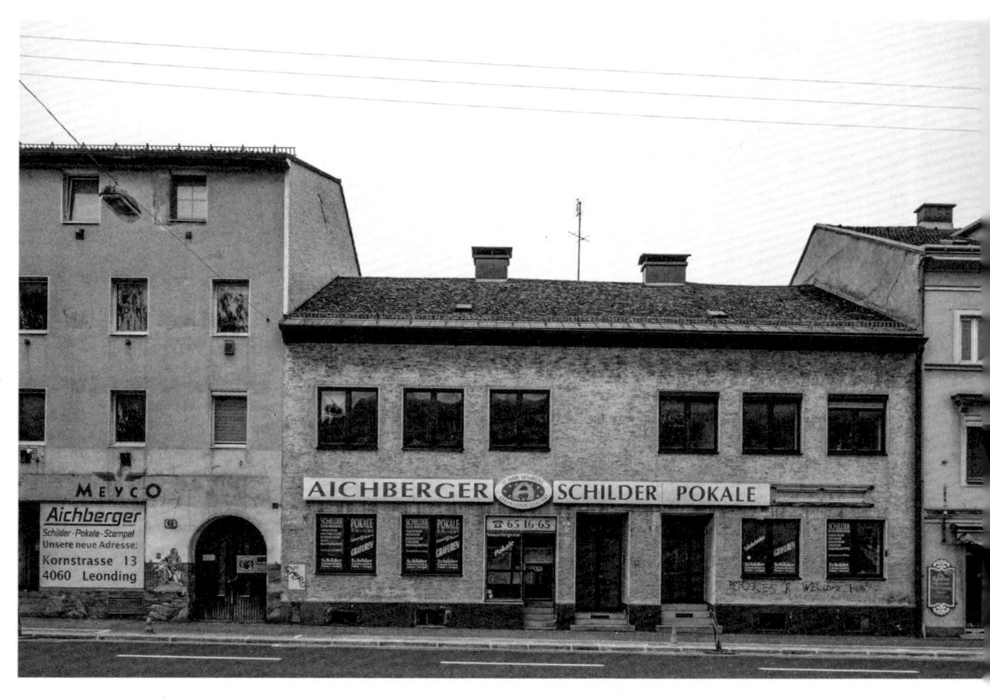
MEYCO
Aichberger
Schilder · Pokale · Stempel
Unsere neue Adresse:
Kornstrasse 13
4060 Leonding
AICHBERGER
SCHILDER
POKALE
65 16 65

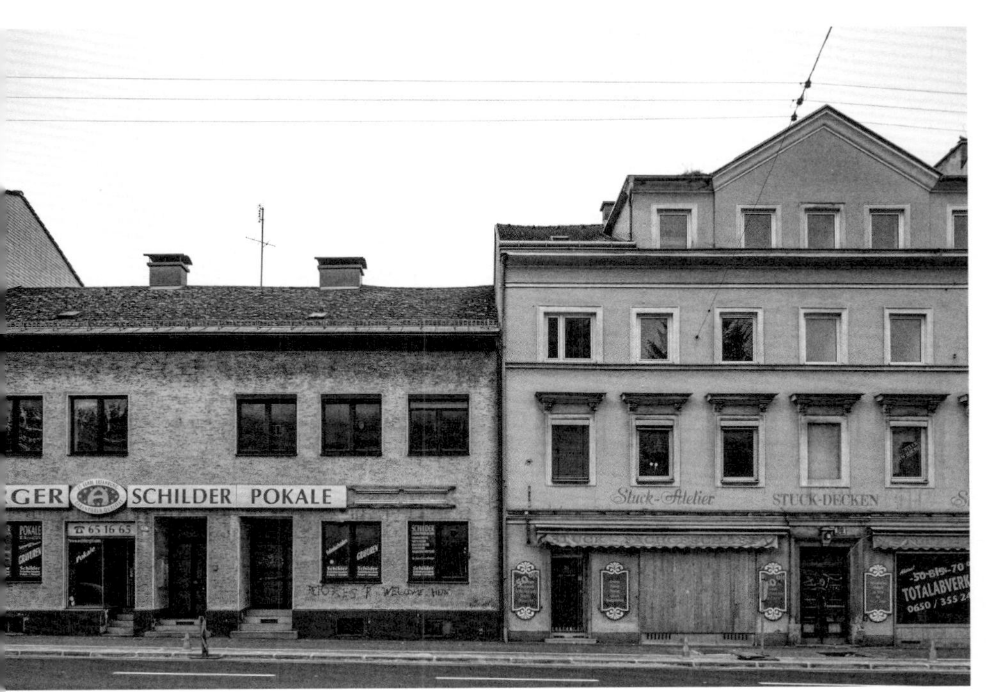
GER
SCHILDER
POKALE
65 16 65
POKALE
GRAVIEREN
Stuck-Atelier
STUCK-DECKEN
TOTALABVERK
0650 / 355 2

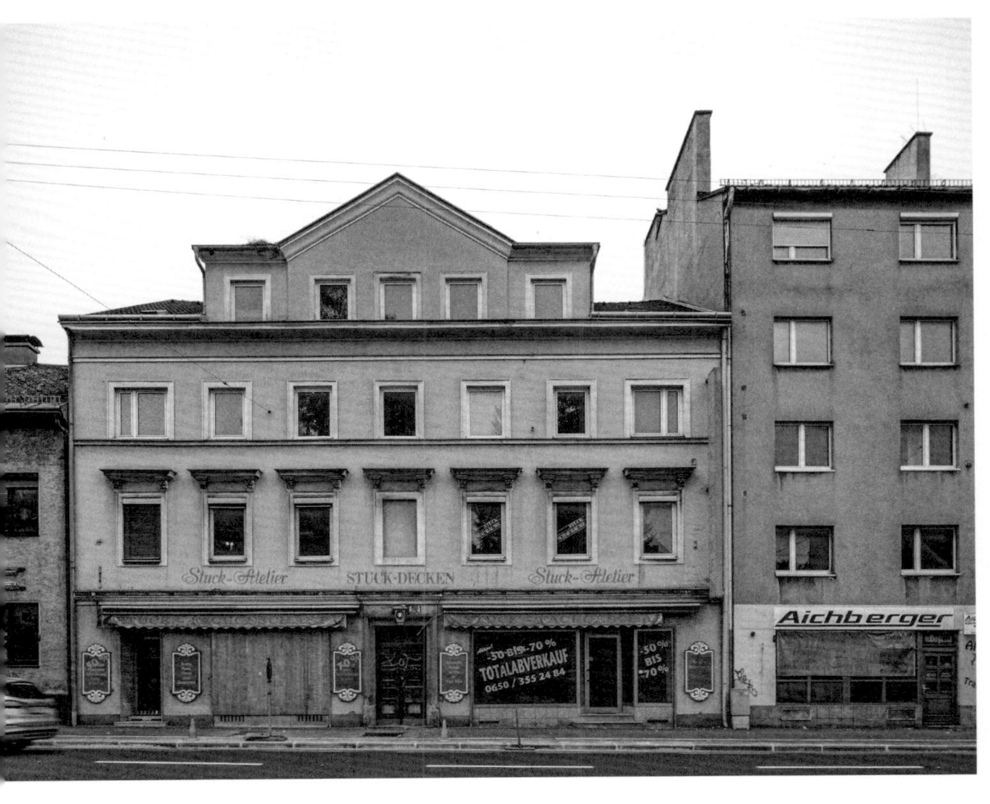

Stuck-Atelier
STUCK-DECKEN
Stuck-Atelier
-50 BIS -70 %
TOTALABVERKAUF
0650 / 355 24 84
-50%
BIS
-70%
Aichberger

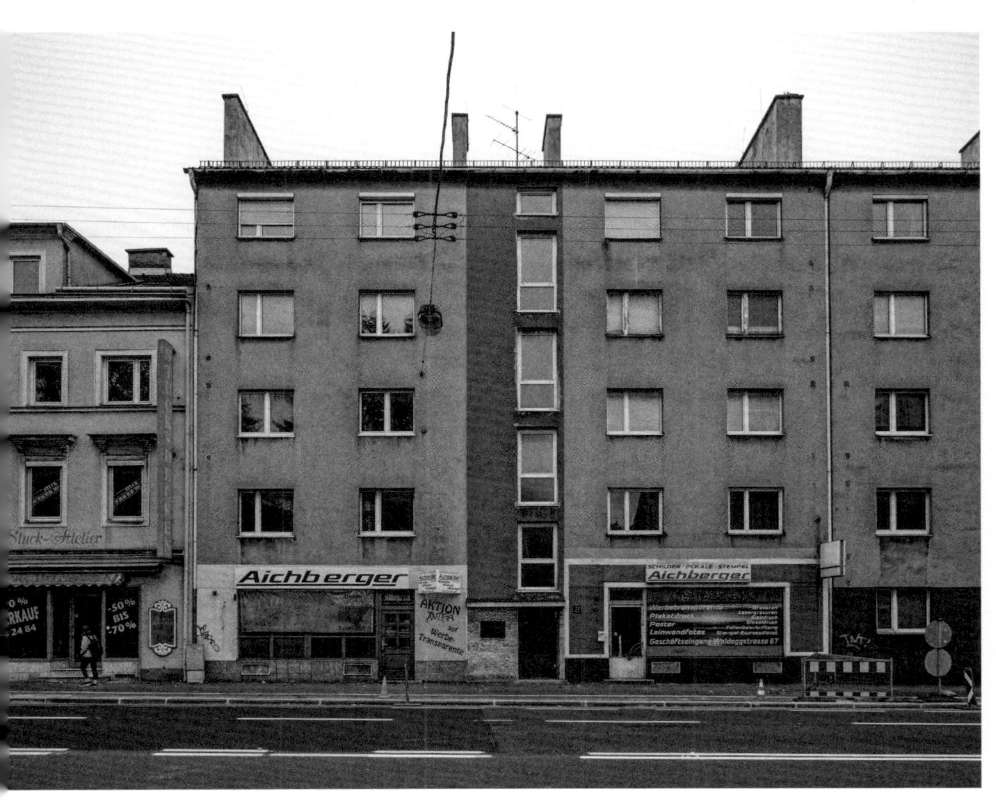
Stuck-Atelier
Aichberger
SCHILDER · POKALE · STEMPEL
Aichberger
Werbetransparente
Plakatdruck
Poster
Leinwandfotos
Geschäftseingang Waldeggstrasse 67
AKTION
auf
Werbe-
Transparente
-50%
BIS
-70%
RKAUF
24 84

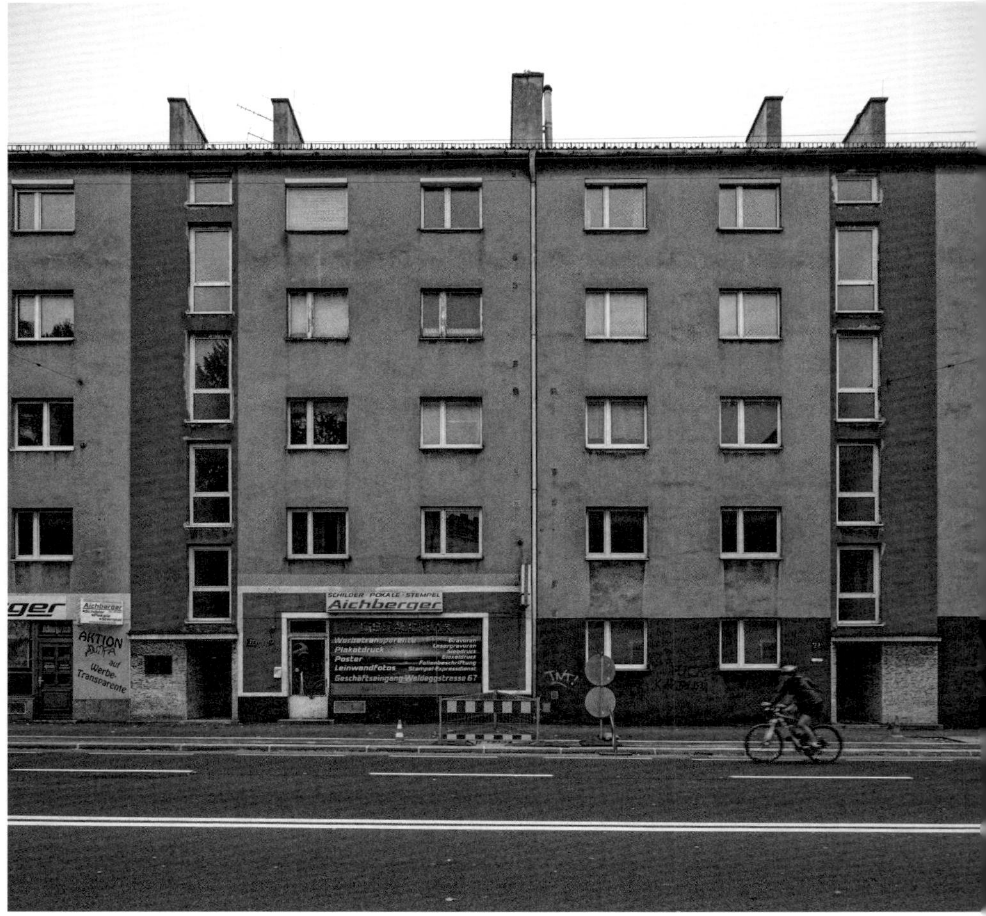
SCHILDER · POKALE · STEMPEL
Aichberger
Werbetransparente
Plakatdruck
Poster
Leinwandfotos
Gravuren
Lasergravuren
Siebdruck
Eloxaldruck
Folienbeschriftung
Stempel-Expressdienst
Geschäftseingang Waldeggstrasse 67
AKTION
ANTIFA
auf
Werbe-
Transparente
Aichberger
»Schilder
»Pokale
»Stempel

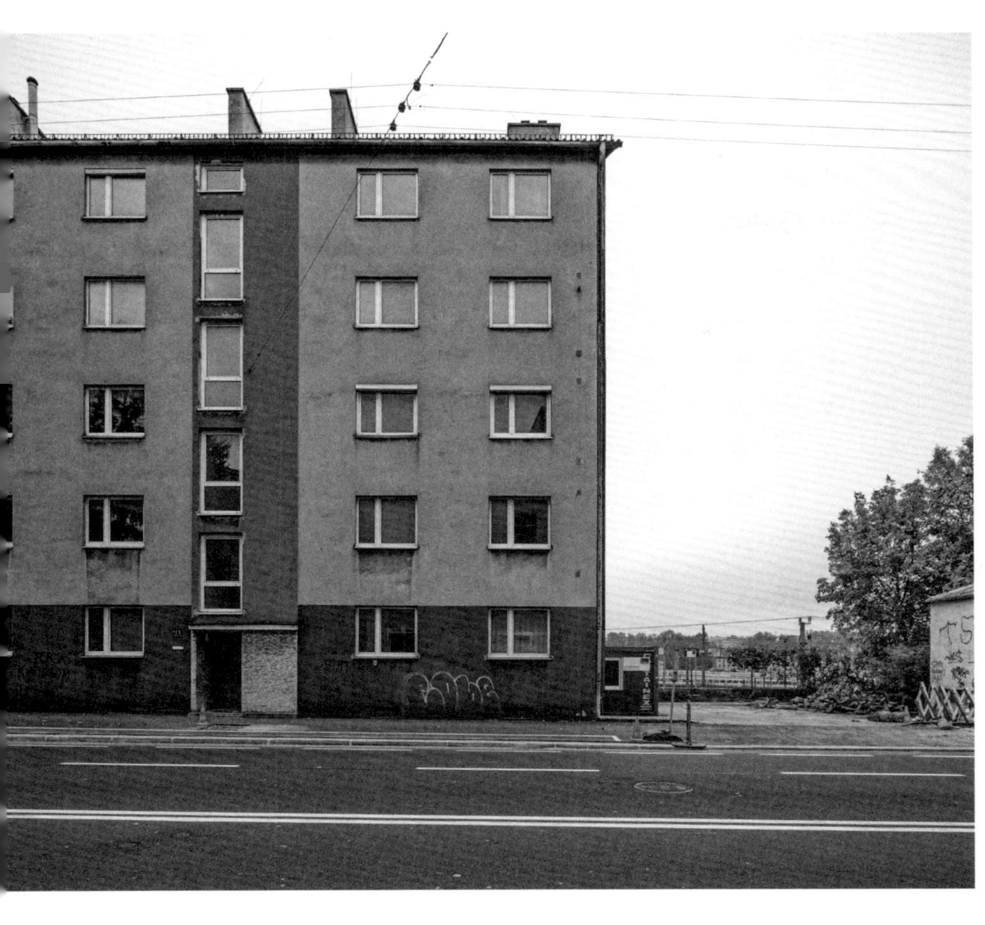

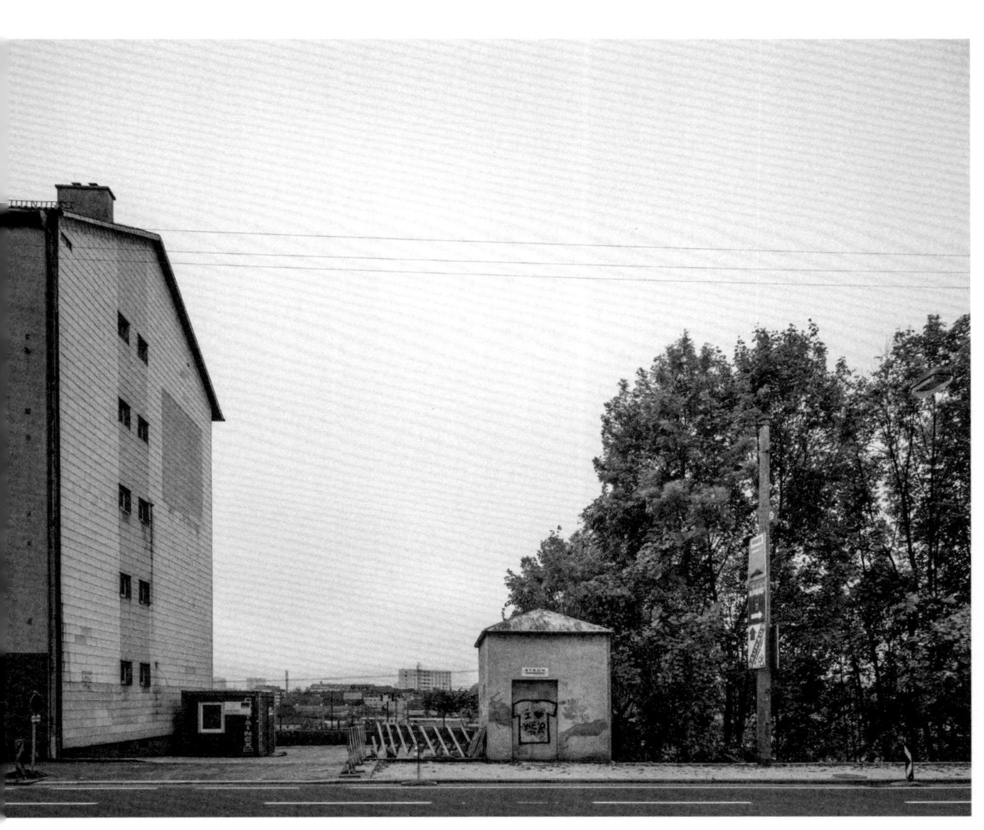